KRYLOV'S BIRDS & BEASTS
A Selection of the Fables

Other books by E. E. Ralphs

TO MAKE A CAT LAUGH

THE CAT IN RUSSIAN LITERATURE AND FOLKLORE

A BEAR BOOK

THE BEAR IN RUSSIAN FOLKLORE AND FABLE

PAINTING THE NUDE

(Translation from the Spanish of J. Parraman)

KRYLOV'S
BIRDS & BEASTS
A Selection of the Fables

E. E. Ralphs

HOWARD BAKER
LONDON

KRYLOV'S BIRDS AND BEASTS

First published, 1990

ISBN 0 7030 0324 0

A HOWARD BAKER BOOK

Printed and bound in Great Britain
and published by
Howard Baker Press Ltd
27a Arterberry Road, Wimbledon
London SW20 8AF

To:
"ALL THINGS BOTH
GREAT AND SMALL"

Contents

IVAN ANDREYEVICH KRYLOV

KRYLOV was born in impoverished circumstances in Orenburg (Chkalov) in 1768, and as a boy narrowly escaped involvement and disaster in Pugachev's rebellion. His first job, as a youth, was in a lawyer's office. He and his widowed mother later moved to Petersburg where he obtained work under the government. He abandoned his position and devoted himself to various forms of undistinguished literary activities, in the course of which he had trouble with the Censorship Department. This he was to recall in some of his Fables.

At the time of Napoleonic European dominance, he finally found his true talent as a writer of Fables. His first book of Fables was published in 1809 and they were at once successful. He was granted a sinecure in the Imperial Public Library, so now he was free to continue inventing more Fables. Apparently Krylov was most at ease in his dressing-gown (there is a word in Russian — *"khalatnost'" which means "dressing-gownism")*. There are echoes of Oblomov in the mental image of the slovenly, gluttonous author, in his dressing-gown, lazily but surely evolving new Fables, with a leisurely zest.

Krylov's popularity gained him Imperial favour; the Empress Maria Feodorovna (knowing how much he loved good food) used to invite him to sumptuous repasts, after which he was expected to "sing for his supper" by reciting his Fables to Her Majesty. She also sent the Royal Doctor to him when he was ill. He died in 1844.

Many of Krylov's fables take the form of the exposure of human weaknesses (particularly of those which are typically Russian) and many are directed against corruption and injustice in the professions, in the government and in official organisations — the sort of criticism which has been levelled at such bodies by satirists since they came into existence. He had, as mentioned above, first-hand experience of the Law and of Censorship, and his victims must have squirmed under the lash of his bitter satire.

No attempt has been made here to follow the vagaries of Krylov's verse forms which, if strictly adhered to, may lead the translator into absurdities and, indeed, into the incomprehensible (see Professor Lavrin's observations in this connection), but rather an effort has been made in these rhyming couplets to give as close a translation as possible and to reproduce the truly Russian spirit of the Fables.

Wimbledon *Dyfed*

One side of the Monument to Krylov in Leningrad

The Fledgling Crow

An Eagle from on high
Down on the flock did fly,
He bore a Lamb off in his claws
Then soared away without a pause.
A fledgling Crow this action saw,
But far from being filled with awe,
"These Eagles must be rather weak,"
He idly thought; "Why soil one's beak
On trifles? In the flock
Is it just lambkins that they stock?
Now I,
If I should try
A foray, home I'd bring
A supper fit for any king."

So high above the Sheep he flew
And took of them a greedy view.
He saw a host of Lambs and Rams and Ewes;
He looked them over, and at last did choose
A Ram — but of all Rams the king,
As fat and strong as anything!
A Ram no Wolf could ever shift —
Downward the fledgling plunged with motion swift
By his white wool he seized his prey
Then saw his plans had gone astray.
Worse still, the Ram possessed a coat so rough —
Tousled and tufty and all shaggy stuff,
Our hero found his claws were tangled fast —
From predator to prisoner he's passed!
The Shepherds freed him from the skein
But so he shouldn't fly again,
They clipped his feathers very short,
Then gave him to their children — for their sport.

. . . .

The same thing happens frequently with us —
It is indeed ridiculous
When petty rogues compete with birds of prey —
They get destroyed — the big crooks get away!

A Train of Carts

A load of pots was carried in a train
Of carts, but steep was the terrain.
    The Waggoner, on reaching a hill-top
    Called on his charges there to stop.
Downhill he led the first cart on its way —
The weight was bravely borne up by the dray.
  At every step that stout old cart-horse made,
  A young horse from above launched a tirade:-
  "Look, what a marvel, what a super steed!
  He scrambles like a Crab, askew, knock-kneed!
    See that? He nearly stumbled on that rock!
    Bravo, another bump, another shock!
The Ass! From fierce abuse I can't refrain;
There! he's turned right instead of left again!
    If he were working *up*-hill, or at night,
Then I'd excuse him — it would be all right;
But *down*-hill leads his path — in broad daylight!
    Such exhibitions make no sense —
    Better draw water if one is so dense.
    But you just watch how *I* make haste,
    Not half a moment will I waste —
My cart will swiftly speed away downhill. . ."
He tensed his spine, with air his lungs did fill,
    He got off to a flying start
    As he rushed downwards with his cart.
    The waggon rolled about and bumped
    As over rocks and stones it jumped;
    It sorely pressed him from behind,
Both back and sides it painfully did grind.
    The Colt went charging on his way,
    With all four legs most gloriously in play.
    Yearling and cart away went bolting,
    Over each rut and furrow jolting.

Down in a ditch he finished, all awry.
 So to all Master's pots — Good-bye!

. . . . .

And like that Colt full many a man I've seen;
To censure others he is very keen.
But when an equal task he undertakes,
Why, then we see just what a mess he makes!

The Geese

A Peasant in a long and straggling train
Was driving once his geese to town, for gain;
And to be truthful, I must say,
He was not over-gentle on the way.
He hoped to profit from them at the mart,
(And when a man has hopes of wealth at heart
Then he becomes a good deal rougher,
And men, as well as Geese, will suffer).
I can't allow the Peasant was to blame;
The Geese, though, had a different frame
Of mind. They hailed a casual passer-by —
To him their Master did they thus decry:
"How could one find unhappier Geese than us?
This Peasant is most barbarous;
He chevies us like any common brand
Of Geese; the fool can't understand
The honour due to us, for we
Are of a famous pedigree.
We spring from that same goosy seed
Which saved great Rome in hour of need;
A holiday is held there in their fame. . ."

"Do you expect to profit from the same?"
Enquired the passer-by. "Why, yes, our ancestors, you see. . ."
"I heard that story at my mother's knee.
But what I'd dearly like to know,
Is why we should respect *you* so."
"Of course, our ancestors saved Rome, we state. . ."
"But what have *you* achieved that you should prate?"
"Nothing!" "Then you're of little worth;
Shut up about your noble birth!
Your fathers' feats gave grounds for boasting;
But you — you're only fit for roasting!"

. . . .

This Fable would be easy to explain —
But that would cause some other Geese great pain!

N.B. Krylov is here deriding the futile and foolish members of the aristocracy.

The Wolf and the Shepherds

A Wolf who near a Shepherd's yard passed by,
Could, through the fence, their goings-on espy.
The shepherds calmly on the head did knock
The Sheep they deemed the best in all the flock.
The Dogs, unheeding, peacefully all lay;
Then growled the Wolf, as, vexed, he turned away,
"Oh, what a mighty fuss there'd be if I,
Not you, had caused that Sheep to die!"

The Lion and the Fox

"What a most terrifying sight!
I really think I'm going to die of fright!"
Thus cried the Fox when first the Lion he saw.
Next time, he felt less overcome with awe;
The third time, he was undismayed,
And with the Lion converse made.

. . . .

We also fear a man of aspect grim
Until, in time, we get quite used to him.

The Boy and the Snake

A Boy once thought he'd caught an Eel —
It was a Snake! He thunderstruck did feel!
With ashen face he stood there in amaze;
The Serpent turned on him her steady gaze.
"Listen," she said, "You must more careful be;
This time, despite your cheek, you go scot free;
God has excused you — but take care
With whom you deal in future — or Beware!"

С. ПАНОВЪ

The Monkey

However hard you've tried,
You won't be glorified,
Nor receive thanks for all your pain
Unless your work produces joy or gain.

. . . .

At daybreak, on his strip of land
A Peasant took his plough in hand
And worked away with might and main;
The sweat poured off him with the strain.
A splendid worker — there arose a cry
From each and every passer-by:
"Well done, well done! You are a brick!"
Such praises made the Monkey sick —
(Applause for others hurts the envious so!)

Therefore, he thought he'd also have a go.
From somewhere he picked up a log
And with it mightily did slog;
He clasped it, rolled it, dragged it round and round —
In floods the sweat streamed off him to the ground.
He puffed and panted — breathless he appeared;
He had to stop — and yet no person cheered!
And that, my friends, may soon be understood —
By mere hard toil you won't do any good!

A Pike

It was a Pike that they to judgment brought
Because so many fishes he had caught.
Those who survived had brought the suit
With ample proofs, and so the brute
In a large bowl was carried into court.
And when the magistrates they sought,
They found them grazing in a near-by field
(The legal records their full names will yield).
They were: Two Donkeys and of ancient jades a pair,
Two or three Goats, and so as to be fair,
And legally quite orthodox,
As the Presiding Judge, they named the Fox.
(With fish, some said, the Pike was able
To add to and enrich the Fox's table).

Great impartiality was shown —
That means, the Pike's misdeeds were all made known.
At length, the hour of judgment came —
The Pike must suffer Death and shame;
He must be hanged upon the nearest tree
And to ill-doers an example be.
"Respected colleagues," here the Fox put in,
"To punish this most vile and grievous sin,
A novel punishment I've found —
Let the wretch not be hanged — but drowned!
This dreadful penalty will surely spread
Among such would-be rogues both fear and dread."
"That's fine!" They all approved the scheme —
They threw the Pike back in the stream.

N.B. Krylov's bitter attack on the Legal System.

Peasant and Snake

Into a Peasant's hut a Snake once wormed his way
And hissed, "Let us be friends, as from this day.
You have no need to fear me now —
I've even changed my looks — that you'll allow.
Just look, in my Spring suit I'm now arrayed!"
The peasant, though, was so hard to persuade.
He seized the Serpent by the head:-
"You may wear your new skin," he said,
"But still an evil beast it fits."
And so he smashed the Snake to bits.

Once you have given reason for distrust,
You'll vainly try the matter to adjust,
But won't atone for your mistake —
Remember then what happened to the Snake.

The Pig

Into His Lordship's yard a Pig intrusively did stray.
Round cook-houses and stables, loafing, he made his
 way;
In dung-heap and in litter he had a happy roll,
Revelling in the sweepings, too, he satisfied his soul.
And tiring of his visit, then
Porky went homewards towards his pen.
"Pray tell me, Piggy-wig, what saw you there,
Rooms full of necklaces and jewels rare?
For that's what all the people here do say,"
Thus asked a Shepherd on the way.
"That only shows what nonsense people talk,"
The Porker answered with a snort.
"I never of such treasures saw a sign,
But as to slops and middens — they were fine!
And yet my snout I've never known to spare —
I cleared that whole back-yard out — fair and square!"

. . . .

Comparisons are odious, I agree,
But surely like that vulgar Swine is he
Who, when he ever criticisms makes,
Ignores what's good and stresses the mistakes.

N.B. This variation of "Pearls before Swine" was Krylov's answer to a piece of unjust and cruel literary criticism made at his expense.

The Swan, the Crayfish and the Pike

When differences occur in an association
No progress can result — but mere vexation.

. . . .

Crayfish and Swan and Pike took part
In trying to drag off a cart.
They harnessed themselves firmly and strove with might and main,
But forward they could never move, for all their care and pain.
Their load was fairly light;
But then, the Swan took flight
Upwards and towards the distant skies,
And all the crayfish could devise
Was backwards to direct his way,
While towards the pond the Pike did stray.
And who was right or wrong is not for us to judge —
But since that day the cart has failed to budge.

N.B. This Fable was explained by President Reagan to Mr Gorbachov at their meeting in the U.S.A. in 1988, as stressing the need for International Co-operation.

The original Fable, however, (written in 1816) satirizes the inability of the Councils and Committees formed under Alexander I to move the heavy load of autocracy and disagreement which prevented them from doing anything useful.

The Squirrel

Below a window in the Squire's dwelling
A crowd of feast-day peasantry was swelling.
They gaped to see a Squirrel in his wheel
Go spinning round and working with great zeal.
Up in a tree, a Thrush was also marvelling at the show,
Amazed to see how fast that Squirrel's paws could go,
Behind him fanning out his tail —
"What do your efforts here avail,
Old friend?" enquired the Thrush,
"Why all this frenzied, hectic rush?"
"Comrade, this vital work fills all my nights and days,
Nor will my Most Important Master brook delays.
I haven't time to breathe, or drink, or eat;
As you can see, I'm run right off my feet!"
The Squirrel started on his wheel again, but faster than before.
"I see," remarked the Thrush as off he flew, "You can't stop any more.

But still up in that window sit —
Forward you haven't moved a bit."

. . . .

Reader, observe some Busy Bee,
Who thinks no man more great than he.
The people are amazed — he bustles round,
But like the Squirrel, makes no inch of ground.

N.B. The fussy, futile official is put in the pillory here.

The Greenfinch and the Pigeon

A Greenfinch in a box-trap once was caught —
He jumped and strove as liberty he sought.
  A fledgling Pigeon mockingly did sneer,
  "What a disgrace! In fullest daylight clear,
    There in a trap you're taken!
    But they would sadly be mistaken
    If they thought me in such wise to take,
    I guarantee I'm far too wide awake!"
    Just then, while he was unaware,
    Himself became entangled in a snare.

. . . .

The moral you'll have guessed, I dare suppose:-
  Beware of laughing at another's woes.

Dog and Horse

Two workers on a farm — Horse and Dog —
Of their respective tasks made out a catalogue.
"Now just look here," said Rover, "your ladyship so fine,
I'd simply turn you out of doors, if you were mine!
To carry, cart and plough is all you ever do,
And nothing else of note is ever heard of you.
How can we, then, our separate jobs compare?
Come sun, come moon, I've never time to spare.
By day, my flocks and herds I guard;
By night, I mind the house and yard."
"Ah, yes," replied the Horse,
"That's all quite true, of course.
But if I didn't carry, cart and plough,
There'd be no flocks or house to guard — as there are now."

С. ПАНОВЪ.

The Feast

In a lean year, to satisfy each beast,
The Lion had arranged a sumptuous feast,
And many a courier did he delegate
To summon every creature, small and great.
And every creature, great and small,
Hastened to answer such a call.
Even in times of plenty, feasts are rare,
And so the Marmot, Fox and Mole went there.
But to arrive on time they were not able,
And found the guests all sitting down at table.
The Fox had much to do that day
The Marmot's toilet caused delay
And the blind Mole — he just mistook the way!
They were unwilling, though,
Their banquet to forego.
They spied a vacant space
Beside the Lion's place;
And there, as plain could be,
Was room enough for three.
"The seat is wide enough, that's true,
Yet," said the Panther, "it is not for you.
The Elephant will shortly claim that place
And quickly shove you out, to your disgrace.
Or worse, he'll sit on you and squash you flat;
I'm sure you wouldn't wish to suffer that!
So here upon the threshold you must stay,
Or, with your empty stomachs, haste away
God bless you, here you may gladly fill your faces
But not in any of the foremost places —
They are reserved for beasts more grand,
For your repast, you lesser guests must stand,
Or else remain at home, in your own land."

N.B. This Fable constitutes a warning to the presumptuous!

The Cuckoo and the Eagle

The Cuckoo once as Nightingale was named
(For this King Eagle's freakish fancy must be blamed).
Proudly the Cuckoo perched upon an aspen tall,
His vocal powers to show to one and all.
He gazed around; and all were taking flight.
Some laughed and others sneered in spite.
Their attitude the Cuckoo sorely pained;
He to the Eagle of these birds complained
"Great Lord," he said, "it was by your decree
That I, within these woods, the Nightingale should be;
Yet they all dare to mock me when I sing!"
"My friend, I am not God — only of Birds am king,"
The Eagle said, "I cannot help you here;
Your title, 'Nightingale' I can command, that's clear;
But make you a *real* Nightingale — that's quite outside
my sphere!"

N.B. This is one of Krylov's digs at incompetent officials.

The Kitten and the Starling

They kept a Starling in a cage —
No singer, he, but very sage.
For long he's had a kitten for a chum —
A kitten — now a half-grown Cat become.
A Cat, though, very mild and meek.
One day, he found his luncheon hard to seek.
They'd quite forgot to give the Cat his food.
Beset by hunger, in distress he mewed. . .
He glumly roamed about, awaiting his repast.
Miaowed and waved his tail and longed to end his fast.
The Starling saw a chance to prate:-

"Dear Puss, you're quite inadequate!
You've had enough of fasting, I suppose?
Why, there beneath your very nose,
There hangs your lunch — a greenfinch in a cage.
You really are a simple personage!"
"But what of conscience?" — "You're not
worldly-wise —
That's all just twaddle, let me you advise.
Only the weak such prejudices feel;
The strong bring everyone beneath their heel.
Here you've a chance this point to prove."
This argument he hastened to improve.
Each philosophic point he brought to light —
The Cat received his theories with delight;
He clawed the greenfinch out — and down he went
Quite tasty, too! But short of nourishment.
This snack left him unsatisfied;
His mentor's teaching he again applied.
Into his cage he broke a hole
And gobbled up his tutor whole!

N.B. This Fable is an admonishment as to what might happen as the result of the influence of vague political theorists.

A Wolf in the Kennels

A Wolf who hoped the sleeping sheep to raid
By dire mischance into the kennels strayed.
The presence of their old grey foe aroused the pack
Of fierce hounds who rushed to the attack
"A thief, a thief!", the whippers-in all shout;
The gates are quickly barred — there's no way out!
All hell has been let loose — there can't be any doubt.
One farmhand with a club comes at a run,
Another pushes forward with a gun.
"Bring lights!", they call, and this is quickly done.
Squeezed in a corner, the grey intruder sits,
Showing his teeth, his eyes reduced to slits;
His hair on neck and back does rise;
It seems he'd like to eat them with his eyes!
But this can not be done while such a pack is near,
And as no further hunting's possible, that's clear,
The sly old reprobate
Determines to negotiate.
So he speaks out: "Dear friends, why, what is this to-do?
I'm your godfather and your kinsman, too.
I come to make a peace, and not to brawl,
The past forgetting and with loving thoughts for all;
Not only will I henceforth leave your flocks in peace,
I'll fight to see attacks on them by others cease;
And on my honour swear, as any good Wolf should...
That I..." — "That kind of talk's no longer any good,"
An ageing huntsman here has his say,
"The hair on both our heads is grey;
You Wolves I've understood for many a day,
And my fixed purpose evermore must stay:-
To peace with members of the lupine tribe,
Unless I've skinned them first, I never could subscribe;

And this will be my rule until I pass away."
He loosed his baying hounds and urged them to the fray.

N.B. The "Huntsman" here is the great Russian General, M. I. Kutuzov. The Wolf is Napoleon who, after the Moscow disaster in 1812, quickly realized his dangerous position and asked for peace. Krylov wrote this Fable in 1812 and sent it to Kutuzov, who read it aloud to his Staff.

Peasant and Fox

A Fox addressed a Peasant thus:
"Friend, we have something to discuss.
How is it that you so esteem your Horse,
For night and day to him you have recourse;
You feed him well; his coat has a fine sheen;
On roads and in the meadows green
I often see you both. But why?
Of all the beasts beneath the sky,
A bigger fool I can't recall."
"That's not the way of it at all,"
The Peasant roared, "I care not for his brains,
But that he'll carry me, obey the reins,
Cart, drag and toil without a slip,
And always answer to the whip!"

Donkey and Hare

A Donkey's not a bird — at flying he's no good;
The one that I refer to thought he could;
And so he boasted, bragged and brayed,
Till all the other beasts he did persuade
That he an aviator was — an ace
Who was the equal of tom-tit for grace,
And high up in the air could rise
To match the Eagle, king of all the skies.
The Hare then said, "Well, off you go, then — fly!"
"Oh, you old cowardly squint-eye!
If I so wished," the Donkey cried,
"I'd soon be up there by the Eagle's side!"
"Well, try, then," the wise old Hare replied.
The Donkey took a run, a skip, a jump,
And landed squarely in a rubbish-dump.

. . . .

Don't ever put on sacred garb — at least,
Unless it happens that you are a priest!

Elephant and Pug

Along the streets an Elephant they led —
Part of a show, of course,
For in our town it must be truly said,
An Elephant's less common than a horse!
A crowd of idlers comes behind him close —
From somewhere jumps a Pug (most bellicose!)
He spies the Elephant, and with aspect grim,
Yapping and barking, hurls himself at him.
"Oh, stop that noise!" the mastiff said,
You, challenge Elephants? You're off your head!
Just look, he onwards makes his way
And will not stay
For all your huff and puff!"
"For me, that's fair enough —
That's what emboldens me," straight came the Pug's
reply,
"Without a fight, I'll make it seem that I
Am fierce enough to take on such as he —
They'll say an Elephant's afraid to spar with me!"

Wolf and Crane

Everyone knows how greedy Wolves can be
And when they're eating, we can see
They stuff down everything — the bones and all
And so misfortune did befall
A Wolf, for in his throat there stuck a bone
So he could scarcely breathe or groan;
His death he could not long postpone!
By happy chance, a Crane was passing by.
By signs and other mimicry
The Wolf showed plainly his distress
And begged deliverance from his wretchedness.
Right down his throat the Crane thrust head and bill
And obstinately wrestled with that bone until
He safely drew it out again: —
Then asked for some reward for all his pain.
"You must be joking!" The wicked Wolf averred.
"You ask for a reward? Ungrateful bird!
Counts it for naught that safely you
Your stupid head and neck from out my maw withdrew?
You just clear off, old chap, and if you're wise,
You'll never more appear before my eyes!"

The Pig Beneath the Oak

Almost to bursting, a Pig one day
Stuffed himself full of acorns. Then down to sleep he lay,
Beneath the parent Oak. On waking up, he set about
Munching the bark and roots with his rough snout.
"That harms the tree, you know,"
High on a branch remarked a Crow.
"If you destroy the roots, the oak itself will go."
"Well, let it wither," says the Swine,
That's simply no affair of mine,
I see no profit in the thing at all,
And quite unmoved I'd see it fall;
So long as there are acorns; see how they make me fat!"
"Ungrateful Pig!" The Oak broke out at that.
"If upwards you would raise your snout,
You'd clearly see, without a doubt,
It is on me those acorns sprout."

. . . .

Ignorant louts are just the same —
Study and learning they alike defame;
Unseeing, while at scholarship they scoff,
That they themselves taste the fruit thereof.

N.B. This Fable was directed at highly-placed members of the so-called intelligentsia who, in Krylov's day, opposed learning and intellectual progress.

С.ПАНОВ

The Lion and the Wolf

One day a Lion on a lambkin lunched,
And while he tore and chewed and crunched,
He deigned to let a pariah puppy stray
Near his repast, and strange to say,
To help himself to several scraps of meat;
The Lion, undisturbed, continued just to eat,
Disdaining with such lowly curs to strive,
And so, unharmed, the pup remained alive.
"That Lion looks so very mild,
I can't believe he's really fierce and wild."
So thought a passing Wolf, and dared put out a paw
To take a piece of meat and stuff it in his maw.
Alas for him, his quite mistaken hunch
Made him an extra to the Lion's lunch!
As he dismembered him, he said,
"You got the wrong idea into your head.
Indeed I rightly spared that wretched pup,
For he is young and foolish — you're grown up!"

N.B. Krylov was once invited to visit a rich and important person who asked him to recite some of his Fables. The poet obliged. The magnate, after listening respectfully, observed, "Yes, that's all very fine, but why don't you write your fables in the style of Dmitriyev?" (The latter was also a writer of verse fables, among other things). "Because I don't know how to," replied Krylov modestly.

But when he got home, he wrote the adjoining. . . !

The Donkey and the Nightingale

A Donkey saw a Nightingale upon a tree,
And said, "Do listen for a moment, friend, to me.
They say that you're the sweetest singer ever heard —
I'd love to hear the voice of such a bird!"
The Nightingale was happy to obey,
And all his glorious talents to display
He trilled in many a harmony, crescendo,
Whistled, then sweetly lowered his voice, diminuendo.
Now like a languid, distant flute he sang.
Now showers of brilliant notes through grove and thicket rang.
And all delighted thus to hear
The voice of Aurora's darling, loud and clear.
The breezes now were hushed — so was the avian choir,
And hushed the nearby beasts in field and byre.
The amorous Shepherd, by his song beguiled
Had ears alone for him, and even at his sweetheart rarely smiled.
The singer ceased his song; the Donkey lowered his head.
"To tell the truth, that's fairly good," he said,
"It's nice enough to hark to such as you,
But you should hear our Cock-a-Doodle-Doo!
If a few lessons you from him could take,
You'd find you would improve, and no mistake!"
This judgment did our Nightingale dismay,
And over many a field he fled away.

. . . .

The Lord protect us from such stupid views, I say!

The Crow

If you don't want to look a fool
Be careful to observe this social rule:-
Don't get ideas above your station
(You'll save yourself such botheration);
Don't try to reach a rank above your own;
If you, a minnow, are among Titans thrown,
Do not think you yourself a giant grown.

. . . .

A Crow who stuck some Peacock feathers in her tail
Hoped some real Peacocks to regale,
As proudly she herself before them bore —
This would her former friends and kindred awe!
Surely to see her in such gorgeous array
Would fill them all with reverent dismay!
The Peacocks as sister her would see,
And soon a jewel in great Juno's crown she'd be.
What was the fruit of all this proud display?
The Peacocks nipped and pinched her plumes away,
And then, when she'd escaped, with much ado,

They'd almost stripped off her own feathers, too.
Back to the Crows, then, but they did not know
This half-plucked bird, and so
They tweaked away what feathers that she had.
The final chapter of her story, then, was sad:-
She'd failed to be a Peacock, as you know,
And now she'd failed as well to be a Crow!

. . . .

This Fable with a story I'll explain —
It came into our Masha's tiny brain
(She was the daughter of a Shopman in our town)
That she could find a spouse of high renown
Because her dowry was so vast.
And Masha wed her nobleman at last.
And then? They reproached her to her face
For being bourgeoise — such disgrace!
So ended Masha's tale of woe —
Neither a Peacock nor a Crow!

The Mouse and the Rat

A Mouse came running up to tell the Rat,
"Friend, have you heard? The Lion's caught the Cat!
Now we can have a bit of well-earned rest
Without the enemy we so detest!"
"Your joy is out of place," the Rat then said,
"For if they've fought, why, it's the Lion that's dead!
The Lion's strength may some appal,
But yet the Cat is mightiest of them all!"

. . . .

I've often noticed, so, no doubt, have you,
The Coward has a corresponding view.
He thinks the man he holds in fear
The rest of us must all revere!

A·L·46

The Lion and the Gnat

It's very wrong to mock the weak,
Or to pour scorn upon the meek.
Beware the vengeance of a feeble race —
Despite your strength, you may end in disgrace.
    The present Fable tells you how
    A Gnat the lordly Lion did cow.
    This is the story that I've heard —
The Lion once a Gnat's great wrath incurred,
    By treating him with cold disdain —
From open war the Gnat could not refrain.
The warrior's trumpet summoned to the field
His foe, who must face Death, or yield.
    The Lion laughs at such a puny beast
The Gnat, though, isn't joking in the least.
    He waits till everything is right
    Then, like an Eagle in his flight,
    First, in the rear he pinks his foe —
The Lion jumps — his tail waves to and fro.
The Gnat's evasive, dodgy, full of pluck —
Blood from the Lion's brow he dares to suck
    The Lion shakes his head and mane,
The Gnat on nose and ear inflicts sharp pain.
    The Lion winced — his teeth he ground
    And tore the earth up all around.
    His roaring made the forest shake
    And all its denizens to quake.
    Who was it that thus froze their blood
    As though they fled from fire or flood?
A little Gnat had caused this fuss and hum —
    A tiny animalculum!
Exhausted by his rage, the Lion falls down flat
    And humbly cedes the victory to the Gnat;
His malice now assuaged, the latter grants him peace.

Homer now plays his part — Achilles' role must cease.
He shrilly sings, as every victor should,
The Saga of his triumph through the wood.

. . . .

N.B. This Fable records the triumph of Public Opinion over an oppressive and powerful government.

The Lion Goes Hunting

Dog, Lion, Fox and Wolf, it so befell
In a rough harmony did dwell.
This was the precept
Which they kept,
That they should go hunting side by side
And equally their booty should divide.
It happened (how and why I do not know)
That once the Fox a fine fat buck laid low,
And swiftly messengers he sent
To let his comrades hear of this event
They soon came running up, you may surmise,
Anxious to share in this most toothsome prize.
Unsheathing his great claws, the Lion took his place
And boldly looked his partners in the face,
All ready to prepare
To grant to each his share.
"Brothers," he said, "We'll cut our lunch in four."
And promptly into bits the stag he tore.
"Now to apportion it — you'll all agree
That by our rules, this piece belongs to me.
The usual Lion's share to me must also fall.
And this — because I'm strongest of you all.
As to this last piece, who would strive
To touch it, surely won't leave here alive!"

The Snake

To Jove a Serpent once made a request:-
With voice of Nightingale he would be blest.
"Or else," said he, "I cannot bear the shame;
The treatment that I get is much the same.
The weak all shun me — and as to the great —
It's only due to luck that I survive their hate.
I'm tired of the afflictions that such a fate can bring;
But if I like the Nightingale with heavenly voice could sing,
Then would I all of them amaze
With admiration they would on me gaze —
My merry talk would everyone enchant. . . !"
Jove was disposed this signal boon to grant;
That odious hiss for ever disappeared —
The Snake then climbed a tree and there upreared,
And sang — it was the very sweetest song —
The birds sat down to listen in a throng.
But when they saw the nature of the singer
His hearers found they had no wish to linger.
Now, who could such a welcome bear?
"How can they spurn so sweet an air?"
The Snake in indignation cried.
"It's not your song from which we hide,
But when we saw your fearsome sting,
It set our hearts a-fluttering,"
The Starling said, "We fear to stay
So near you. If you keep away
We'll gladly listen to each glorious note —
But only at a distance far remote."

Ass and Peasant

A Peasant with a vegetable plot
An Ass as warden for it did allot,
To safeguard every useful plant that grows
From flocks of thieving sparrows and of crows.
The Ass was of the truest kind,
To greed and pilfering quite blind —
Never a leaf of Master's did he harm,
But kept the feathered tribe in great alarm.
But from it all came little gain —
With all four hooves the Ass lashed out amain
To scare the birds, but in his haste,
All garden produce he laid waste.
For up and down and right and left he tore
Destroying vegetables by the score.
The Peasant then was quick his wrath to show,
And on that Donkey's back showered many a blow.
"He got what he deserved!" I hear you cry,

"It's not a Donkey's place to try
Such uncongenial work to undertake!"

. . . .

I don't support the Ass, make no mistake:
His master was quite right to make him ache.
But should the Master not himself be blamed
Who for such work a Donkey named?

N.B. The above attacks incompetent government officials — and the Head of the State who employs them.

Speckled Sheep

The Lion, Speckled Sheep could not abide
He could, of course, have stooped to genocide;
Such conduct, though, would sully his renown —
Unworthy of the bearer of the crown
Which he, as King of Beasts, had every right to wear —
(His duty — to protect his subjects and their lives to spare).
And yet, those Speckled Sheep preyed on his mind!
How to destroy them, yet appear most kind?
So he convoked the Bear and Fox
To help him solve this paradox —
The sight of Speckled Sheep gave him such awful pain
His eyes, he thought, would never bear the strain;
He feared the risk of going blind —
No answer to his problem could he find.
Frowning, the Bear spoke up: "Almighty King!
I find it easy to resolve this thing —
Just give the order, without more delay,
All these unwanted Sheep to slay!"
The Fox, seeing the Lion scowl,

Addressed him in a humble growl:
"No doubt, my gracious King and Lord,
You mercy to these creatures will accord
Innocent blood I'm sure you'll never shed —
Would you consent to hear my plan instead?
Grant to them many a luscious field,
Which forage to the Rams and Ewes will yield,
With room for Lambs to play and jump for joy.
And as few shepherds we can now employ,
Ordain that Wolves the flocks should guard.
It seems to me, in this regard,
That, anyhow, the Sheep are dying out
And soon will be extinct, no doubt.
So let them have a good time while they can —
Whate'er befall — you're not the guilty man!"

And it was so successful that, at last,
Not only Speckled Sheep became quite few,
But ordinary White Ones, too!

N.B. Krylov, perhaps wisely, did not submit this Fable to the Censorship Department (which he criticises in some of his Fables). It was found among his papers after his death and was originally written at a time when the Universities were suffering violent repression and persecution. The Lion here, as in other Krylov Fables, represents the Tsar.

(See "Cat and Nightingale" in "The Cat in Russian Literature and Folklore", by E. E. Ralphs, published by Charles Skilton: also other Fables in that volume).

The Wolf and the Young Mouse

A grey Wolf, straying from the pack,
Once dragged a Sheep upon his back
Into the woods, and in a sheltered nook,
His guest he all to pieces took
And with such zeal and gusto lunched
That one could hear the cracking bones he crunched;
But, glutton as he was, he couldn't eat it all —
Some he put by, and then to sleep did fall
After his feast. While thus he lay
It chanced a Mouse now came that way,
By such delicious odours drawn
O'er hillock and through prickly thorn
He crept, seized on a scrap and went
Back home again — impenitent.
Later the Wolf his loss could plain descry;
He raised a noisy hue and cry —
"Stop Thief and Brigand, Help!" he sobbed,
"My hard-won savings have been robbed!"

. . . .

I saw such an event in town today;
Our Justice's gold watch they stole away.
And loudly he expressed his grief:
"Robbers and Brigands! Help! Stop Thief!"

N.B. The above reflects Krylov's views on the legal profession!

С.ПАНОВЪ.

The Hare Goes Hunting

The animals had gathered in a group
And off to hunt the Bear the gallant troop
Went out, and in the plain
Their poor victim soon lay slain.
Now came the time for each to take his share —
The choicest bit was snaffled by the Hare.
"Where have you sprung from?" other hunters cried,
"During the hunt, we thought you'd gone to hide!"
"But listen, friends," exclaimed the Hare,
"You surely must have seen that I was there?
Was it not I who drove our quarry from the wood,
Enabling you to settle him for good?"
This boastful talk, though none were taken in,
At least among the huntsmen raised a grin;
And so the Hare his cherished place did win.

. . . .

And so, although the Boaster makes us smile,
He often wins rich prizes through his guile.

The Cock and the Pearl

One day, while rummaging about the midden,
A Cock scratched up a Pearl, which long had lain there hidden.
He crowed, "What have we here?"
A useless thing, at which to sneer.
"What fools men are so highly to esteem it, —
To my mind nothing can redeem it.
I would prefer, myself, to find a grain of rice;
On that I set a higher price;
For though it's very small,
It's good to eat, withal!"

. . . .

Thus ever thinks the man of understanding dim —
He finds no good in anything which is no use to him.

The Sheep and the Dogs

For the protection of a flock of Sheep,
And so that they in peace could sleep,
No longer fearful of the Wolf's dread raid,
In watch-dog numbers they an increase made.
So what? The pack had soon so multiplied
That every Sheep in safety could abide.
But Dogs, too, find they have to eat;
After the wool was stripped, they took for meat
The Sheep themselves, and sad to tell,
Their numbers under double figures fell —
The Dogs then ate up those, as well.

N.B. In this Fable, Krylov directs his criticism against those Government Departments which are so overcrowded that the ordinary civilian population itself is outnumbered and pushed out of the way.

The Cuckoo and the Cock

"Friend Cock, how loudly and how grandly you do sing!"
"And sweetly, Cuckoo, in my ears your lovely voice does ring.
There's not a singer in our wood
Who would not emulate you — if he could!
Whene'er you cease your dear melodious strain,
I want impatiently for you to sing again.
For me, that such a voice could be, seems strange —
So pure, so tender, and with a soaring range!
You can't be called outstanding, as to size,
But Philomel herself your voice would prize!"
"Thanks; and *I* find your song more charming and precise
Than of the heavenly birds who sing in Paradise!"
A Sparrow overheard them in his flight,
And thought that he would put them right.
He said, "You may praise each other till you choke,
But still your tuneless music's just a joke."

. . . .

How can the Cock so flatter, without shame,
The Cuckoo, with his dubious fame?
Because the Cuckoo treats him just the same!

Monkey and Glasses

A Monkey grew short-sighted in old age.
Men were at hand his fears to assuage.
They said, "This difficulty's easily resolved;
A pair of spectacles — and your problem's solved!"
A dozen pairs he promptly bought,
But vainly tried to wear them where he ought.
He twisted, turned them, stuck them on tail and head;
He sniffed them, licked them — all to nothing led.
"To Hell with them!" the angry Monkey cries,
"Only a fool would listen to men's lies.
They urged me to waste money on these glasses,
But never said they's be no good to me — the asses!"
In grief and rage he seized the glasses all,
And dashed them quite to bits against a wall.

. . . .

Unfortunately, men are equally to blame:
Things of most worth to them, they treat the same.
The ignorant on all such treasures spit,
And if the clown's a really first-class twit —
Why, then he makes an end of it.

The Miser and the Hen

The Miser covets everything — he loses all,
And many examples I could now recall
(But that they slip my lazy mind)
But here is something of the kind:-
A Fable dating from long, long ago;
When I was still a child they told me so.

. . . .

A man once lived who knew no craft or trade,
But daily in his chests fresh fruit he laid —
A Hen this enviable person had
Which daily made the greedy miser glad;
For it laid eggs of an unusual mould —
Not just the common sort, but solid gold!
Now most of us would be at peace
To see our wealth so easily increase.
But this was not enough for him;
The Miser nourished a most curious whim;
He thought that if the wretched fowl he killed
It would with golden treasure all be filled;
Although the bird had brought him such delight,
The sense of gratitude forsook him quite;
He chopped the Hen to bits — for this offence
A heap of entrails was his recompense.

The Frog and the Ox

A Frog once in a meadow spied an Ox,
(She was both envious and unorthodox),
And undertook a daring enterprise:-
To equal him in burliness and size.
And how she huffed and puffed and blew!
She said, "Dear Croaky, tell me true,
Do I approach him yet?"
"Not in the least, my pet,"
Replied her slimy friend. "But yet you must agree,
I'm swelling vastly — that you must surely see?
No? Well, then, what of this? Have I not matched him now?"
"You couldn't match a Lilliputian Cow!"
"Well, this then?" "You are just the same."
And in the end our comic envious dame,
Failed in her effort, however hard she tried,
And, overdoing things, exploded and so died.

. . . .

Such cases among men are not unique,
When every little bourgeois sneak
And all the gutter-bred small fry
To emulate the gentlemen will try.

The Spirit of Inquiry

"Hello, how are you? Tell me where you've been?"
"In the Museum — the marvels that I've seen!
I looked at everything with scrupulous care,
I simply can't describe the wonders there!
In every chamber miracles abound —
I'm sure that nothing like it elsewhere could be found.
What new inventions will Dame Nature next devise?
Such birds and Beasts of every sort and size!
Such tiny bugs, such beauteous butterflies —
Insects so small they quite deceive your eyes.
Some like to emeralds, some to corals seem —
And little lady-birds; I deem
A pin-head must seem vast to such as they. . ."
"And how about the Elephant? They say
He is so very large and stout —
You thought you'd run into a hill, no doubt?"
"You mean the Elephant is there?" "That's right."
"I never noticed him — a tiny oversight!"

N.B. This Fable, written in 1814, is based on fact. Krylov heard of a visiting provincial gentleman who acted and spoke in the way described above.

The Lion in Old Age

The mighty Lion, woodland's fearsome King,
Was close to death, and now lay languishing.
Those terrible sharp claws and fangs were blunted now
Which once the fiercest enemy could cow.
His feeble legs could scarcely bear him on his way,
But to worse ills he soon became a prey.
For now, each once-insulted, vengeful beast
No longer found him awesome in the least.
They heaped upon him insults, pain and woe;
First, the proud stallion's hoof inflicts a blow
See where the tooth of Wolf has made a rent!
A wound from Bullock's horn is here quite evident.
The wretched Lion, near his final breath,
Awaited but the final smart of Death.
And only by a weak and hollow roar
Could he his miserable fate deplore.
But when he saw a Donkey make his pick
Of where he best could hurt him with a kick,
"Let me not suffer such disgrace,
O God," the Lion groaned, "Let me embrace
Grim Death at once, for with his sting
He surely could not greater torture bring,
Than those which from a Donkey's insults spring!"

The Fox

'Twas early on a Winter's morn —
There, at an ice-hole, stood a Fox forlorn,
Quenching his thirst — Unluckily it chanced
His tail into the gelid pool advanced:
The ice seized on the tip and froze it there. —
What matter? This was easy to repair.
One mighty tug would free him of the snare,
Leaving behind a strand or two of hair. —
Then off back home while men were still asleep.
But could he hold his lovely tail so cheap? —
That gorgeous tail of goldy, fluffy down?
Perhaps he'd wait a bit — still sleeping was the town —
And then, perchance, there'd be a thaw:
Then from the trap his tail he could withdraw.
He went on waiting — his tail the ice held fast —
He saw that darkness would no longer last.

The World was waking up — the sound of men came
  clear.
    The Fox now wildly struggled, mad with fear,
    But now that icy grip he cannot break.
    He saw a Wolf and cried, "For Heaven's sake,
    My dear old friend, help me in my dire need!"
    This passing Wolf gave to him timely heed.
        He hastened to his comrade's aid,
        And quick work of his task he made:
        Off that fine tail he cleanly bit —
        That was the long and short of it!
    I think this Fable's meaning is quite clear:
        The loss of sundry hairs is not severe —
It's losing life itself which you must fear!

N.B. This is one of Krylov's fables directed against the Censorship.

The Master and the Mice

If in your house you think thieves are around
And yet no evidence of them can be found,
Be careful how you charges make of theft,
Or wildly punish suspects, right and left.
That's not the way to catch your thief,
Nor bring to you the least relief;
You'll only make good servants shun your door
And land in greater trouble than before.

. . . .

A merchant built some warehouses one day
And in them various foodstuffs stowed away.
And to prevent the Mice from doing any harm,
He wisely bought some Cats to serve him as gendarmes.
Mice could no longer him dismay —
Feline patrols went out by night and day,
And all seemed to be well
Until it so befell
A thief among the guardians did appear,
(For among Cats and Police this can occur, I fear);
And so, first catch your thief and hold him tight,
But justly treat the guiltless, as by right,
This merchant's verdict was more rash:-
He threatened every Pussy with the lash!
On hearing of a sentence so severe,
All Cats, both good and bad, did disappear;
And to the Mice the way was left quite clear
To carry out their greedy plans and schemes,
And to fulfil their cherished hopes and dreams.
Catless the barns — into the stores they went,
And ere three weeks were fully spent
They'd eaten all the nutriment.

Dancing Fish

(1st Version)

Complaints about the strong, the rich, the law —
The Lion found the endless stream a bore,
And so set off himself his lands to scan
When he arrived, he saw a countryman
Who'd lit a fire, some Fish he's caught to fry
The Fishes did their best to jump up high
In the hot pan, seeing their end was nigh,
Yawning and gaping in despair.
"What are you doing? Who goes there?"
The stern and fierce Lion roared.
The awestruck Peasant said, "O Lord,
I am the Bailiff here, these fishy folk to guide,
And these are elder Fish who in the depths reside.
Great King, we're all assembled here
To welcome you with many a cheer!"
"And in this region, is there aught they miss?"
"My Lord, they pass their lives in everlasting bliss.
We pray you'll live for ever, if you can!"
(Meanwhile the Fish were throbbing in the pan).
The Lion asked, "But, tell me, pray,
Why do they wag their heads and tails that way?"
"They find your presence so entrancing
That joy has set them all a-dancing!"
They parted: the Lion by mere chance
Upon the dancers gave a final glance
Before proceeding elsewhere to advance.

This illustration appeared in a selection of Krylov's fables for children published by "Detskaya Literatura" in 1983.

Dancing Fish

(2nd Version)

As sovereign of the woods, and of the waters, too,
The Lion summoned, as his due,
The Beasts, in order to prescribe
A ruler for the finny tribe.
A Fox was thus elected to the place
Of Governor of the piscine race.
He noticeably fatter grew —
Among the country folk he knew
Was a firm friend. Together they
Produced a scheme for capturing their prey:-
While on the bank the Fox dispensed the law,
His Peasant hauled the Fishes to the shore.
Then, like good mates, they portioned out their catch —
Yet the rogue one day must meet his match.
The Lion heard a sad lament:-
That in some local government
The law was being vilely bent.
He chose the most convenient day
Then off he started on his way
This province for himself to scan. —
There on the bank he saw the Fox's man
Who'd caught his Fish — his fire was going fine;
He and his partner soon might grandly dine.
The Fishes did their best to jump up high
In the hot pan, seeing their end was nigh,
Yawning and gaping in despair.
"What are you doing? Who goes there!"
Fiercely the angry Lion roared.
The cheat replied, "O Mighty King and Lord!"
(The Fox has always ruses ready)
"This man's my faithful secretary.

He's famed for honest dealing far and wide —
These Carp beneath the water all reside.
Great King, we're all assembled here
To welcome you with many a cheer!"
"And are all happy here? In law, is aught amiss?"
"Lord, here all pass their lives in everlasting bliss.
We'd have you live for ever, if you can!"
(Meanwhile the Fish were throbbing in the pan).
The Lion asked, "But tell me, pray,
Why do they wag their tails and heads that way?"
"They find your presence so entrancing
That joy has set them all a-dancing!"
Such lies the Lion could not stand,
And, as all dancing needs a band,
He made good use of tooth and claw,
And forced those villains both to sing and roar!

N.B.
During one of his journeys round Russia, Tsar Aleksandr I stopped at the house of a Provincial Governor. When he was preparing to leave, he saw through the window a fairly large number of people approaching the house. On the Tsar's asking what this signified, the Governor replied that it was a deputation of the people coming to thank His Majesty for the prosperity of the region. The Sovereign, in a hurry to get away, declined to receive them. Word went round later that they had really come to complain about the Governor, who, incidentally, later received an award. At that time, military oppression had led to revolt among the settlers, but yet the Tsar was assured that, "Thanks be to God, peace and happiness reign everywhere."

The Censor suppressed this first version of the Fable which was not published until 1869. The second version differs in so far as the Fox (as the cunning man in power) appears and, above all, the ending has been fundamentally altered, so that the guilty are punished, whereas in the first version the Lion passes on without noticing anything.